*Sue . I
enjoy the
of poems*

*John P
24/6/19*

Lyrics & Lines

by

"Carolus"

"These lines do not pretend to emulate
The mazy verses of a mighty master;
In their defence suffice it if I state
They are but fancies of a poetaster."

Grosvenor House
Publishing Limited

First Published in 2019 by Bollin Publishing Ltd.
ISBN 978-1-78623-476-6
Copyright 2019 © Bollin Publishing Ltd.
Copyright 2019 © Lyrics & Lines
Illustrations by Jacqueline Tee

A CIP record for this book
is available from the British Library

This book is produced by
Grosvenor House Publishing Ltd
Link House
140 The Broadway, Tolworth, Surrey, KT6 7HT
www.grosvenorhousepublishing.co.uk

Website: bollinpublishingltd.uk
Email: bollinpublishingltd@gmail.com

In Memory of the
       Happiest Days
             of my life

and

To the guiding spirit
       of those swift but
    ever to be remembered moments
    these feeble efforts are dedicated

C. F. W.

FOREWORD

I had owned the handwritten manuscript, a small hardback notebook, a gift from a now deceased cousin, for some fifteen years until I actually opened and read it. Since I am not really interested in poetry it had sat unread on a bookshelf until one day I decided to look at it properly. From the first page I was hooked and read on, finding myself entrapped by its messages of love and sorrow, history, legend and the macabre. **Lyrics,** when expressing his emotions, **& Lines** for the remainder seemed an appropriate title.

"Carolus", who was he and when did he write this? The one clue as to when written, the only date in the book, was '1905' but in a different hand.

From the humour of "Lapsus linguae", "Riddle" and "To Let", moralizing under "Keynsham Bridge" and the black thoughts of "A Vision" written in the style of, and reminding one of, Dante and his 'Inferno', I felt that this as yet unpublished work should see the light of day and be made available to all.

It was, I suppose, written as a gift to a loved one, the intensity of the love poems and the feeling of having been rejected or having lost whomsoever 'she' was is,

I found, compelling. Love, humour, wisdom, and his macabre thoughts tend, at least to me, to make the narrative a most unusual present for a loved one. Perhaps it was for a lady whose name started with an 'O' - "My Programme". My cousin's Mother-in-Law was called Olivia and she married in 1906.

Having read this book I would hope that all would agree, that described by himself on the title page of this book as it being '*but fancies of a poetaster*', "Carolus" must have been a very modest man.

JPP Feb/2019

Poetaster - A person who writes inferior poetry OED.

INTRODUCTION

The author of this 'Love Offering' of poems remains unknown.

Who was he, When and Why and Who were they written for? Where did he live?

With such intensity of Love, Humour, and why so poignant and again Macabre?

Who was "Carolus"?, his pseudonym, mediaeval Latin for Charles, maybe is a clue as to who he was. "Further Lines in an album" where he signs off with a "C" adds weight to perhaps Charles ... and why did this Charles wish to hide his real identity?

Where did this Charles live? Maybe, deduced from two of the longer and perhaps more historical offerings, in an area of the County of Somerset to the South of Bristol. Both "Keynsham Bridge" and "The Legend of St. Keyna" are set on the banks of the river Avon as it wends its way north towards the City of Bristol and thence to Avonmouth and into The Bristol Channel.

When was he there? An addition to the main manuscript, and written in another hand is an extract from Robert Hitchins tale *"The Garden of Allah", Read at Saltford, August 1905*, probably written by an elocutionist. This then provides us with an indication of the early 1900's making him a contemporary or maybe even a friend of Thomas Hardy.

Why did he write this collection, and why under a pseudonym? It is clear from his dedication and "L'Envoi" which concludes these 42 unpublished poems that he intended to give them to a Lady - maybe he did, maybe he didn't. We just don't know so there the mystery remains.

Index

"Amor l'incomprehensible"

Love is a butterfly, gay as gay,
A moments' passion, a lifetime's sway;
Sipping the sweets of a blossom here,
Tasting the tempting nectar there;
Flitting about and caring nought,
Happier e'en when soonest caught;
Love is a butterfly, gay as gay.

Love is a fancy, swift and strong,
That fears no hurt, and knows no wrong;
Fancy free, till a willing thrall
To a kindred heart's ecstatic call-
Love that for love had briefest died
Sooner than have its love denied;
Love is a fancy, swift and strong.

Love is a paradox, strong men bend
Among the weakest: love will lend
A strength undreamed of to the weak,
Make Dumb the bold, the silent speak;
Dull the wits of the foolish wise,
Give to the blind a lover's eyes;
Love is a paradox, barely kenned -

Love is a Trinity of the three,
At variance all, yet all agree;
Not to be gained by sight of gold,
Priceless, love is not bought or sold -
Still without love the world would die;
Paradox, fancy, butterfly,
Love is a Trinity of the three.

----o----

Fragment

*L*ove is a flower to droop and die
By wintry tempest blighted;
But hard the heart that can deny
A flaming love while lighted.
The Vestal Virgins' ceaseless watched
The fires upon their altars;
And cupid's dart when once despatched
Upon its course ne'er falters.

Those altar fires had burnt away
And swift have had an ending
But for the Virgins' day by day
Perennial zealous tending.
So love will everlasting burn
If love reciprocating,
But will it never callous turn
If slightly long kept waiting?

----o----

Viola

Soothe me, my Love,
my soul with stanzas steeping,
Breathing of love, thy face to mine inclined;
Rock me, my head upon your bosom sleeping,
Around my neck thy tender arms entwined.

Lift up thy voice, my Love and sweetly warble,
Carol a song than nightingale more clear;
Soft let me kiss thy throat as white as marble
That shyly tells thy love into mine ear.

Look in my eyes, my eager gaze delighting,
In mine reflection of thy pure face see;
To further rhapsodies of love inciting,
Yielding to Cupid's sweet philosophy.

Tho' worlds my clash, Time still be onward moving,
Death unto others all too present seem;
We for each other our affection proving,
Twin souls, will glide thro' life in endless dreams.

----o----

"Phyllis"

A line in this book to you, Dearest, is due,
Tho' small is the need your perfection to praise;
For none to your charms any question could raise -
He who follows his nose,
Could at once if he chose
Through life in his heart bear a picture of you.

----o----

"My Programme"

*T*he letter "O", your Christian name's
Initial, of some twenty places
Upon my tiny programme claims,
I notice, quite a dozen spaces -
To think of scandal do not deign,
Since we enjoyed those dances so;
For others let the task remain
Of counting and exclaiming .....O!

----o----

To "Aimée".

"A steed, a steed, my Kingdom for a steed"
In accents frenzied once exclaimed a King,
Calling aloud his men a horse to bring
To serve his master in his pressing need;
Small value for a throne must he display
Who thus so lightly gives a crown away.

A heart, a heart, I ask thee but a heart,
A love eternal equal unto mine;
Take, take my love, and in exchange for thine
Unite, unite the two no more to part;
My love indeed to me is no more use
If you my pleading lightly should refuse.

I give my heart away without a thought,
I swear to thee my love will e'er be true;
Then do not scorn my suit or make me rue
The telling on't by setting it at nought;
So let your love around my heartstrings twine;
Be you my own, let me be only thine.

----o----

"Lapsus linguae"

If from me when my lips you have kissed, sir,
A kiss in return you have wrung;
In defence of myself I insist, sir,
It was only a s...lip of the tongue -.

----o----

To a Lady Cyclist

Ah maiden Mine,
With form divine,
And manner most entrancing,
I see that you
Now cycle too,
And limbs and life are chancing.

The angels may,
(well, so some say,)
Be excellent creations;
They may have wings
and other things,
To help in their gyrations.

Of course you must take this on trust,
I can't help but assume it;
If better men believe it, then
T'were rude to not presume it.

Swift as a bird,
I've always heard,
The angels are in flying;
But when you ride,
To keep beside
You, they would soon stop trying.

Wherefore about
You go, without
An angel guarding you, Dear;
This some regret,
But they forget
That you're an angel too, Dear.

For you, my Dear,
Have naught to fear
From Pharisaic leaven;
You could, no doubt,
To all point out
The royal road to Heaven.

I know full well,
You can excel
The angels in your graces;
Your beauty's frame,
In utter shame
Would make them hide their faces.

But if your past
May have been fast,
Your future will be faster;
(I've prophesied
The way you'll ride,
Not social disaster.)

So by your side,
I too will ride,
That is if you'll endure me;
My fears you ease,
And one more lease
Of life you do insure me.

May every joy
Without alloy,
Be yours where'er you're spinning;
And God forfend,
You lack a friend,
Until to death you're winning-

----o----

A Riddle

My brain with this riddle is riven,
Just think how it muddles the head;
Tho' a pen may be easily driven,
A pencil is best when it's lead.

----o----

Helen

*T*hou rulest me - Ah! glorious eyes
Wide open with a coy surprise
From out them beaming - Thine the frame
Worthy of everlasting fame -
Mark how each man when first he spies
Thy angel form in wond'rous guise,
Prostrate in adoration lies;
The while he murmurs still the same
Thou rulest me!

Scarce do I dare e'en to surmise
Thy soul responsive to me sighs,
Or that without thy love it dies;
Didst thou not oft so sweetly blame
My heart for being worldly wise -
Then who can scoff, as loud it cries,
In answering accents to my claim,
Thou rulest me!

---- o ----

"To Let"

I'm looking around me, midst girls that
surround me,
For one who will be a companion for life;
A maiden to cheer me and to her
endear me,
In fact who will make me a dear little wife -
I see you are winking, perhaps you
are thinking
Amongst so much beauty I'm most hard to please;
But how can I marry, unwedded I'd tarry,
If I had to marry such maidens as these?
Maids that are frigid, with backs that
are rigid
As pokers, or prudes who are out on the
prowl;
Maidens with eyes that grow wide with
surprise at
One's slightest advances, and stare
like an owl.

Maidens pedantic, with trilbys gigantic,
Such as you see on the Salvation Sals;
Maidens who ever just seem to endeavour
To talk of naught else but of dress & fallals -
Maids with a mission, who seem an addition
To church & to tea fights but wouldn't suit me;
Maidens whose faces would frighten the Graces,
And rival the Gorgons, as plain as can be -
Maidens athletic, with limbs energetic,
Caring for nothing but horses and dogs;
Maidens from college, quite chock full of knowledge,
With minds but for books & for stern pedagogues.
Maidens who giggle & try hard to wriggle
Themselves to your heart by their simpering ways
Maidens who glare at you, nay! almost
swear at you,
If you don't humour their favourite craze -
Maidens who're simple, perhaps have a dimple,
And every atom of sense quite without;
Maids who are haughty, maids who are naughty,
Maidens who always are gadding about.
Maidens so tall that they seem to see all that
Passes, while looking far over your head;
Maidens who please you, but possible freeze you
With glances that make you skedaddle instead-
Maids whose complexions may seem quite
confections,
'Till you find out they rub off on your sleeve;
Maids who are tearful, and maidens so cheerful
That nothing at all ever seems them to grieve.
Maids who're all honey, so long as you've money,
But when you lose it will give you the shove;
Maidens ecstatic, who'd live in an attic,

At least so they say, if they had but your love -
All are quite willing a place to be filling
As wives, but their own imperfections forget;
So then I'm waiting, just this one fact stating,
Here's a young man who is well ...er..
"To Let"

<u>Reply</u>
As you only speak of maidens let me soft suggest to you,
That a charming little widow as your spouse perhaps might do.

----o----

To "A Friend"

"A friend in need is a friend indeed"
Is a maxim old and true;
Even the rankest growing weed
Protects the drop of dew
That lies beneath its slender shade
Against the Sun's fierce glare;
Even the humblest friend, dear maid,
Can keep the heart from care -

Then let me call myself your friend,
Be you the same to me;
Permit me like the weed to bend
That I may shelter thee -
Then may you like the dewdrop pass
Secure from harm through life;
As flower within a house of glass
Shut off from care and strife.

---- o ----

On a Drowned Girl

Drowned! Can this be death? So calm a face
Seems rather to nestle in sleep's embrace -
Who, without knowing, would have supposed
Those eyes for ever and ay were closed?
That last the smile that her lips doth wreath,
Those lips that never again will breathe?
But the erstwhile throbbing heart is still,
The body - beyond all human skill -
Drowned indeed, while the spirit has fled
Her body one of the countless dead -
Amazed in truth was the passer by
Who chanced far down in the depths to spy
Of the river bed that form so fair,
The shroud composed of her jetty hair -
Peering, peering in wondering awe,
His eyes aghast at the sight they saw,
Marvelling whether this frame serene
A living maiden ever had been;
Or whether a Nereid fast asleep,
Insensate lay in the water's deep;
But glancing again he pitying found
T'was the corpse indeed of a maiden drowned-
The river weeds, in their cruel sport,
With their strong embrace her limbs had caught,
But seeming to feel, too late, regret,
Now nursed her soft in their swaying net -
While leisurely past her flowed the tide,
Swinging her gently from side to side;
Like a mother her child unto her breast
Rocking, compelling the babe to rest -

So she lay, 'mid the cradle of grass,
The waters a requiem as they pass
Murmuring; Vision divine by death
Kissed, and his kisses stilled her breath -
To answer her call no help around,
In her youthful vigour & springtime,
"Drowned" -

---- o ----

Spoken by a Skull

*M*ark my jawbone's evil grinning
At the living round me sinning;
My poor soul has had to pay
For the passions of the clay;
Shortly it will be the turn
For ye who gaze on me to burn -

. . .

I had feelings such as yours,
Sinned I just as many hours;
I atone in death the sins,
Your dread day is still to come -
Your poor whit upon me play,
Rue it at some future day.

. . .

Does my gentle jibing smart?
As I was so thou now art;
As I am so thou will be,
A mass of grim inanity;
Thinking of your load of sin,
In irony compelled to grin.

. . .

Mark my hollow cheeks and eyes,
Fancy that you hear my sighs;
My poor skull in truth confirms
The pleasures down among the worms -
Treat me gently - Thank my stare
If it reminds of Death. - Beware!

---- o ----

Reflections

*L*o! Another Year has hurried
Past and joined those long departed,
Such the speed at which it scurried,
That t'was o'er ere scarce it started.

Hark! the bells crash from the steeple
Heralding the New Year's coming;
Like myself how many people
Are the past year's actions summing?

Thinking of their joys and troubles,
Of their eager toil and strivings;
Of their hopes dispelled like bubbles,
Of the dead and of the living -

Far into the future gazing,
Longing for some revelation;
Buoyed, sustained by hope amazing,
Though but scant its information -

Making resolutions brittle,
Scarce performed and quickly broken;
Sometimes kept when mentioned little,
Soonest dashed when soonest spoken -

I myself make no delusion
Or pretence of soul ablutions;
This my motto and conclusion,
Dash all new year resolutions!

---- o ----

What Matters?

The last leaf on a withered tree,
Link t'wixt life and eternity,
Shrivelled and swept aside 'twill be;
What matters?

Trees as fair in myriads grow,
Leaves as green will bloom and blow,
Care they nought for another's woe;
What matters?

The last puff of a cigarette,
Its dying watched with deep regret,
One lingering longing thought, and yet,
What matters?

Thousands more with their fitful glare
Will sooth the troubled mind from care,
Then fragrant be dispelled in air;
What matters?

The last hope in a failing cause,
Should it succeed, the world's applause,
But fails it, wolves loud ravening roars;
What matters?

Many a hope forlorn has won,
Many have failed ere scarce begun,
'Tis but the web that fate has spun;
What matters?

The last day of the dying year,
The past may slide, the future clear,
Or death remind his time is near;
What Matters?

Years have vanished and years will go,
Bringing their train of weal and woe,
History's stream ne'er stays its flow;
What matters?

The last breath of a dying man,
Whose sands have run, whose lifetime's span
Has fallen 'neath Death's remorseless ban;
What matters?

Thousands lie deep beneath the sod,
Thousands are but an earthly clod,
Thousands have gone to face their God;
What matters?

The last man on the earth alive,
The last bee in the world's vast hive,
Mad fears and doubts his senses drive;
What matters?

Tho' last of all men, in his frame
There rests the whole world's sin and shame,
Thousands before have found the same;
What matters

The last soul on the Judgement Day,
Awaiting sentence, afraid to pray,
Cursing the sins of his mortal clay;
What matters?

Myriads of souls have pardon craved,
Myriads the purging streams have laved,
His but last to the damned or saved;
What matters?

---- o ----

To a Lady on the slaughter of her pet canary by her cat

She speaks........

*I*n the slough of despond, in the depths of despair,
In handfuls and handfuls I tear out my hair;
My heart is distracted by sorrow and pain,
While a queer sort of feeling encircles my brain.

I weep and I weep, while my tears flow in streams,
And my sleep is disturbed by disquieting dreams;
I mourn all the day and I weep all the night,
By the time I have finished I shall look a fright!

Perhaps you will wonder what terrible trouble
Has ended my pleasure as bursteth a bubble;
It pains me to tell you, but briefly 'tis that
My darling canary's been poached by my cat.

What terrible anger my breast madly burned
When the cage of my treasure I found overturned;
But a far greater horror my heart turned to stone
On finding my lovely canary was gone --

I sought in each room and I sought on the stairs,
I sought 'neath the tables, the piano, the chairs;
But all that I found was one small gory stain,
And I feel now I never shall see her again;

That cat must have eaten her feathers and all,
For the trace that she left was so terribly small;
A suitable punishment now is the question,
If I beat her I only shall spoil her digestion -

Here's a curse on that cat, may her teeth tumble out,
May she hardly be able to hobble about;
May her claws shrivel up and her eyes become blind,
And I hope no more pleasure in life she may find.

Ah! how sad now I feel; oh! I wish I could die:-
When I do catch that cat won't I make her fur fly!
But one consolation I grant you is given,
I trust I shall meet my poor darling in Heaven

---- o ----

A Vingt Ans

*T*o jog along jollily always gay,
With nobody caring to say you "nay",
While shines the sun let all make hay,
　　Hurrah for ease and plenty;
But what will come of it some may say,
You know there'll be the devil to pay;
　Well every dog must have his day,
　　At least at the age of twenty-

---- o ----

Lines in an album

*T*he calf that was nurtured 'neath
fair summer skies,
Would have prayed from his life to be free,
Had he known that his highest ideal would
be reached
In belonging entirely to thee -
Could his greatest ambition or notion of bliss
Be more than to cover an album like this?

In fact had he known as he went to his death,
He would even have fondled the knife;
And as he expired with his last fleeting breath
Have blest them for taking his life -
I too (you permitting) these sentiments feel;
Did I not then my heart would be harder
than steel -

The delicate leaves which these covers contain,
What tales of their past could relate!
Transformed from a rag or a duchess's train,
Till they've now reached their acme of fate -
For what greater honor could fall to their share,
Than to keep all these signs of our love in their
care?

Perchance I write nonsense, perchance I write truth,
Perchance I write something of each;
My words may be foolish, my verses uncouth,
But spare them a glance, I beseech -
Should you give but one thought to the words
I have said,
Then this book and myself are both amply repaid.

---- o ----

Further lines in an album

Dear Kittie, perhaps you remember you asked me
To write a few lines to adorn this fair page;
So I'm doing my best, but I fear you have tasked me
Beyond my poor powers, for I'm not quite a sage -

Tho' I own that these verses cannot, without bragging,
With lives of a laureate poet be classed;
Yet still in the future, should mem'ry be flagging,
They'll serve to remind you of pleasant days past.

Perhaps you'll be married, your lifetime enjoying,
For of you I can prophesy nought but the best;
And I hope that no trouble will be you annoying,
But with all the good things of this world you'll be blest.

And then as you scan them you may perhaps wonder,
(That is if you think of the writer at all;)
As to whether I've risen, or if I am under
Like so many others, and gone to the wall .

I too may be married, with bairns young and healthy,
Which alas! to success are as so many clogs;
Or perhaps have got on and become almost wealthy,
Or poverty stricken have gone to the dogs -

Forgive me for scribbling this maudlin effusion,
But the past has been sweet as a long summer's day;
I probably cherish a foolish delusion,
And the future may bring many seasons as gay -

My excuse must be this, that I oft times remember,
While my heart is rent open with many a spasm,
'Twixt the springtime of May and the chills of December
How great and how terribly wide is the chasm -

Whatever may happen, how e'er far we're severed,
I hope still a friend and a true one I'll be;
To be such indeed I have always endeavoured,
And as such I will sign myself:
Ever yours:- C. ..

----o----

Lines in a Confession Book (from which some pages are missing)

"Confession is good for the soul, dear"
You said as you gave me this book;
And I started, but thought on the whole, dear,
I'd stop after taking a look -

For I see that the leaves you've been thinning,
(And the same to my page may befall!)
So it seems not much use my beginning
To write a confession at all -

Since if I write down here each failing,
Each hope, aspiration, each fear;
It does not appear much availing,
If the page from the book you should tear.

Forgive me for speaking my mind, dear,
Should these verses your feelings enrage,
The remedy easy you'll find, dear,
'Tis simply to tear out this page!

---- o ----

Habit

What habits man is subject to!
When from my slumbers I arise,
The first thing that I always do
    Is rub my eyes.

Then if I chance to be perplexed,
And what I want I cannot find,
Or angry grow and very vexed,
    My teeth I grind.

Supposing that I moralize
Upon this world of care and sin,
And sudden feel most wondrous wise,
    I stroke my chin.

And then if ever I should feel
The leaden weight of dark despair;
This is the way my woes I heal,
    I tug my hair.

Should anyone, in metaphor,
My nose put out of joint, suppose,
As though my real one was sore,
    I smooth my nose.

But if I feel that I am blest
With every comfort, joys complete;
I lock my hands upon my breast,
    And cross my feet.

And after dining ere my brain
To sleep's refreshing call succumbs,
From thought distracting to refrain,
I twiddle my thumbs.

If cramp should seize my limbs in bed
My aching leg I softly nurse;
And lest I utter words ill bred,
My lips I purse.

I hate by any to be chid,
And as my habits now I've sung,
I'll stop, lest anyone should bid
Me hold my tongue.

---- o ----

Apology

Our paths which erstwhile met now separate,
And sad indeed each lot, how sore each heart!
The bony fingers of an unkind fate
Our lives doth part -
Thou sayest, ere I loved, I should have scanned
My future, lent my ear to warning calls;
But what man fears the Damoclean brand
Before it falls?

----o----

My Valentine

Come Cupid closer to me here,
And listen do whilst in your ear
My tale of love I'm pouring;
Don't shuffle so upon your toes,
And lead me ever to suppose
That you perhaps I'm boring -

I fondly love a darling maid:
Now do be still, I'm half afraid
That you are callous growing;
You turn a deaf ear if you dare!
Within her heart love's seeds with care
Have I been eager sowing -

You seem to think you've heard before
Of angels like her by the score,
But ne'er before or after
Is maid with face and form so fair,
Such eyes, such grace, such glorious hair;
Such ripple in her laughter -

To gaze upon her is a feast
Ah far far greater at the least
Than yet vouchsafed to mortals;
I ask you, lad, to pour your darts
Within the mazes of her heart's
(I trust me) willing portals -

No feeble words of passioned praise
Could tell my feelings as my gaze
upon her form first rested;
The gods themselves no words could find
To tell the glories of the Kind
With which her face is vested -

My boy, I'm sure where'er you've been
You never in your time have seen
Two eyes more true and tender;
No language could express her grace,
No word the beauty of her face,
Her wondrous charms could render -

Now boy, for me a message bear
To her, forget it if you dare,
And mind you do your duty;
Just tell her that I suppliant crave,
To be for evermore her slave,
In thrall unto her beauty -

What's this? your duty plain you shirk,
And you refuse to do this work
Which ought to be a pleasure;
Well then I'll ask it her myself;
Go, leave my sight, you foolish elf,
And rue your sins at leisure.

----o----

Amoris Sententiae

*H*ow sweet how sad the thoughts that flit unending
  As spirits thro' the watches of the night;
Souls long since reft once more their greeting sending,
  Faces long lost appear again in sight.

I hear one voice when hushed all else is seeming
  Thrilling amid my heart's increasing gloom;
Message in hope in passioned phrases streaming,
  That ne'er may be fulfilled this side the tomb -

I feel a hand my fingers interlacing,
  As once I knew in days long since so well;
Magnetic touch all bygone woes effacing,
  Causing my deadened heart to leap and swell -

Two tender eyes my orbs so weary meeting,
  Welding our souls in unison once more;
Yielding unasked their clear tho' silent greeting,
  Dearest, I love thee and adore.

I feel two hearts against their portals leaping,
  Stirring as one to soar for ever free:
All, all in vain, I sink in anguish weeping,
  Ne'er but in thought I shall belong to thee -

---- o ----

To a lady going to Siam

*T*hough our English land will miss you,
And though everybody's heart
Will now contain a vacuum
Where once you were a part;
Yet while good wishes follow you
It's thinking more, I am,
Of the everlasting honor
You'll confer upon Siam

---- o ----

Dead

*L*ost to me, torn from my arms by death,
With querulous plaint my heartstrings seethe;
Why in the midst of our happiness
Should she be taken, and I alone
Be left to follow where she has gone?
To mourn the years that I have to pass
Till the sands have run through my lifetime's glass,
Ere in death I feel her soft caress -

Few but the days that our souls communed,
And our hearts in love's sweet strain were tuned,
Till death unstrung with a boundless rift-
She is no more, but mid earthly pains
A hope of heaven at least remains;
Constant I know her spirit awaits
My tardy coming at Heaven's gates;
Death which will be Life's greatest gift -

---- o ----

"Adio"

Say not goodbye my fairest! dry thine eye,
Let not those pearls so clear and dewy fall;
Take heart of grace, and cease to wonder why
Fate tears me from thy loving arms at all -
Say not goodbye! six moons, my own,
Will to their full be gaining
While I am absent, six alone
O'er both our heads be waning -

Absence, my dearest, ever has been said
To knit two hearts together nearer still;
As to thy faith to me naught do I dread;
My love for thee will last thro' good and ill -
Will not our souls as oft before
In realms of dreams be meeting?
Will not our hearts untrammeled soar
O'er myriad miles in greeting?

But half a year has swiftly by to slip,
While afterward what hope the future gives;
'Tis but as if one single drop should drip
From out the glitt'ring ocean of our lives -
Say not goodbye! Each day will make
our union ever nearer;
Each hour that passes will but wake
A love that grows but dearer -

----o----

"Cause and Effect"

That dance! if I remember rightly
We sat it out behind a screen;
A shaded lamp shone none too brightly,
Indeed your face could scarce be seen -
You asked me if I liked your dress,
But as 'twas dark I had to guess -

We were, I think, then eating ices,
The while you waited my reply;
I thought 'twas one of your devices
To make me feed on humble pie -
A simple "yes" or "no" I knew
As answer to you would not do.

I knew your dress was very charming,
Of all the ball you were the belle;
But still your question was alarming,
The kind of stuff I could not tell -
You must have seemed to all delightful,
Since every other girl was spiteful -

But how can man however willing,
Of gussets, fichus crêpe, or tulle,
Of chiffon, pongée, moiré, frilling,
Pleating or gores discuss in full -
These are beyond his intellect;
He only views the whole effect -

Long gloves of kid or suéde, and clocking
Upon a dainty ground of silk
That made with open work a stocking
Through which your skin shewed white as milk -
This last I managed just to scan
On stooping to pick up your fan -

Then next there met my downward gazing
A glacé kid or satin shoe,
Embroidered, buckles brightly blazing
And bronze, (or was it pink?) the hue-
It really was so very small
I hardly caught a glimpse at all -

Your hair was waved; I wonder whether
By tongs or Hindes or crimpoline;
Your ..... well in fact, your altogether
To me seemed worthy of a queen -
At least it caused me to discover
How much I longed to be your lover -

I really tried to do my duty,
My answer by you was not scorned;
I murmured I believe that beauty
Was best when it was unadorned -
You married me, and now I pay
For things like those you wore that day -

---- o ----

Her Birthday. (actali 21)

*H*er Birthday! Come poetic muse
Thy pen with language fit infuse;
Teach her to every wish I send
A heedful willing ear to lend -
What shall I wish her? Health and Joy,
Wealth, even love without alloy
Have all grown hackneyed; all mankind
Have wished the same, e'er since the mind
Was first created; from that day
It has occurred to all to say
The self same words; then how can I
In different terms aspire to try
To utter wishes with my pen
Which have eluded other men?
I must then feebly follow suit
By hoping that the golden fruit
Of all you long for, all you want,
May come to you, a débutante
Upon life's stream; You have begun
(Since you today are twenty one,)
Your first experiences of life,
Its struggles, disappointments, strife;

As for each worldly purpose you
Have been an infant hitherto -
By this, in truth, I do not mean
That you till now a child have been
Except within the legal rule;
(Of course you say "the law's" a fool,)
And I agree; it does indeed
Seem foolish that a child be freed
From all his debts and actions done
Until attaining twenty one -
But what I really want to say
Was that with you now lies the way
In which you choose your life to shape;
For you it now remains to scrape
From off your future's face the dust,
And rub it clean of spot or rust -
With you alone the chances are
Whether your life you make or mar -
You hold the scales within your hands;
You cannot see the yellow sands
That drip unceasing through the glass
Of time; how soon your life will pass
Away to you is hid, so spend
Your life so well that at the end
The weight of good within the scales
At once may show that good prevails -
Then let me wish, then let me hope,
That life for you will always slope
In pleasant prospect; every hill
Become spreading plain at will;
That life its joys in goodly store
Around your onward path will pour,
And every day by you be passed

In pleasures greater than the last -
Your heart untouched by carting care,
Your life as light as mountain air;
Your steps in pathways pleasant placed,
Your form with every beauty graced;
Your life a stream of endless bliss,
What more then can I wish than this?

----o----

To a Former Friend.

How wondrous Nature's workings are that circle us around,
The earth, the sea, the skies above, the marvels underground.
'Gainst Nature's everlasting rule the puny power of man
Has small effect; What can he do within his life's brief span?
The sun his daily course will run till swallowed up by night,
The moon will shine, the stars above shed their endless light,
The wind will blow, the rain will fall, the seasons come and go,
What then can man e'en at his best against such forces do?
The tides will ebb, the tides will flow, the world go on forever,
But Death steps in and ends for man his uttermost endeavour.
So I must love you evermore tho' you my love may scorn,
I cannot help if in my heart such love for you be born;
My will is sunk beneath my love, but if you bid me cease
To love, you only cause my love to all the more increase -
Time will go on eternally, Death's power be at an end;
My love will still remain should you my very heartstrings rend,
Then oh be kind, and strive I pray to bend your heart to mine,
And be to me a loving friend, as I am wholly thine -

---- o ----

Rejected

A phrase rang in my ears at night
As t'were some broken heart's wild call;
"T'were better to have loved and lost
Than never to have loved at all"-

And long I pondered o'er the words,
And thought of that which might have been
If I had known you long ago
Before another came between -

A second phrase I seemed to hear,
"With each how happy could I be",
I cast it from me with disgust,
As some vile beast one loathes to see.

This second is the filthy brood
Of some debased and sordid mind,
Which treasures lust within its heart,
And round it like a serpent twined -

He never knew the power of love;
Poor fool! how empty is his soul!
But lust incarnate beats supreme
Through all his pulses like a ghoul -

But he or she who've really loved,
But yet alas! have loved in vain,
Have tasted heaven's undying gift,
Though earth has intermixed her pain .

And if as friends they still remain,
True loving friends in every sense;
There's still a taste of heaven for each,
And "Honi soit qui mal y pense".

----o----

Eternal Love

Canto I

--- o ---

'Twas Eventide, and the twilight grey
Was mourning the death of another day -
The full moon rose and all nature slept,
Whilst a wonderful silence reigned, except
In yonder coppice, the mournful strain
Where the nightingale sang her sad refrain -
The Drowsy bee at length was still,
The wheel was stayed in the old grey mill -
Perchance I slept, in troth I dreamed,
Of a wonderful love that truly seemed
Impossible. Suddenly lovers twain
Before me stood; the like again
I ne'er shall see; The maid more fair
Than mortals ken of, light as air
She tripped the sward, and by her side,
With an arm encircling his new made bride,
There strode a youth with a hero's mien,
And the haughty look of a god, I ween -
I looked in their eyes, and lo! I saw
A love that I ne'er believed before
Come welling forth, so pure and clear,
Like a crystal stream when the spring is near -
It spoke of a love so deep and true
That was made with the world, and would I knew
Last on for ever, Ay! so complete
As would even the power of death defeat -
And I saw it had passed through many a strife
'mid the toils and cares of this mortal life;

Full often oppressed and cruelly used,
Misunderstood and by some abused,
It had lived to vindicate its name,
Proclaiming far its immortal fame,
Unruffled, unmoved by worldly cares,
A wonder at which the whole world stares -

End of canto I

---- o ----

Canto II

*T*he vision passed, I relapsed in sleep,
But awoke again from the slumbers deep
To dream once more; and I seemed to see
The self same spot, but in some degree
The scene had changed; it had older grown,
And I instantly saw that Time had flown
On his eagle wings, and had left his mark
On the glassy glade and the mossy bark -
And as I looked o'er the rugged scene
Which in years gone by so fair had been,
There rose before my startled gaze
The lovers again amidst the maze
Of brushwood. Time had lightly dealt
With each, but all the same I felt
That with hearts as true and hand in hand
They were drawing nigh to 'death's' borderland -
I sadly thought of the days of yore,
When hope was high and the years before;
But I saw in their eyes the same bright gleam
Of unquenchable love, like one long dream
Of unending happiness, steady and bright
As the stars above, or the harbour light

Which guides to the haven of rest at last,
With the journey done and the dangers past -
And as I gazed, on my awestruck view
A figure appears betwixt the two,
As I looked on his form, I held my breath,
For I felt in my heart 'twas the longed for Death,
Who had come at last on his mission dread,
To number the lovers among his dead.

End of canto II

---o---

Canto III

*T*he scene had changed - In a noble nave
I stood by the side of a simple grave -
As sadly I gazed I thought with pain
Of those who within the tomb were lain -
With tears in my eyes I slowly read
The words on a stone placed overhead;
"These two whom no trouble or care could move
Have lived and died in undying love."

----o----

"Keynsham Bridge"

By yonder bridge which spans the Avon o'er,
Whose mighty arches stretch from shore to shore,
I chanced to wander once in careless wise,
Content alone to muse and moralize -
Halfway beneath an arch a pathway leads,
Slippery with slime and rankly growing weeds;
A massive stone all future progress bars,
Covered with moss and many dents and scars -
Some trails of ivy round it loving fall
And struggle upward clinging to the wall -
Above the bridge there lies an ancient weir
O'er which the waters dash in mad career,
Churned into foam and mist with endless roar,
As ever onward through each arch they pour -
A placid stream the Chew, as fast they roll,
with sluggish courses multiplying the whole,
And instant past each pile together crash
With eddying whirlpool, sullen swirl and splash -
Onward the water dashes, madly on,
Here for a moment, then forever gone;
Bursting against the vast supports that rise
Unmoved in massive columns to the skies -
Pieces of driftwood, twisted, twirled and tossed,
In mad confusion pass, and then are lost -
Such was the varied scene as by the stone
I stayed to muse and moralize alone -
I heard the carts move slowly overhead,
I heard each footfall, every passers' tread;
I watched the waters' rapid onward flow
And likened them to life, its weal and woe -

How often life's long rush compared has been
To all the varied views and change of scene
Of some vast river; first the bubbling source
Unwitting, careless of its future course;
Then gaining strength and haughty in its might,
Fast plunging onward, eager for the fight:
Then later on with broad and placid face
It sober glides within the banks' embrace;
Till last of all it gains the mighty sea
And there is lost for all eternity.
Such thoughts passed through my mind as if a dream
Of life's eternal rush and endless stream -
I sat till Even; soon a silence sank
On all around; The scene grew dim and dank -
I heard the lowing of the cows afar
And watched the rising of the evenstar -
My thoughts went back to days of long ago
With all the martial glory, derring do -
I thought of how upon this very bridge
The rebel Monmouth's troops from yonder ridge
Had met King James's men, essayed to cross,
And duly beaten been with dreadful loss -
I pictured to myself the scenes of war
Enacted there in days so long before;
The battle cries, the fight, the gasping breath
Of wounded warriors going to their death;
The clash of steel, the cannon's sullen roar,
The erstwhile peaceful scene bespilt with gore;
The battle shocks, the heavings, cursings, groans,
The victor's triumph shouts, the dying moans -
Whilst musing thus I sudden passed my hand
Unconsciously beneath an ivy strand,
And started forward in amaze to feel

The prick and clammy cold of rusty steel.
My first brief wonder o'er I felt anew,
And from its age encrusted shelter drew
On old world sword, its blade and hilt with rust
Thick spread by time and damp in ruddy crust -
Upon its ancient form I looked amazed,
Yet rubbed its blade unwitting as I gazed -
And lo! before my startled eyes there grew
These letters written, first of all a few,
Then more and more, till presently I read
This line which stretched from rusty point to head;
These were the words, "Capio et vivam do",
"At my command life's stream will ebb and flow",
"At my command to death a life I give,"
"At my command I cause a man to live"-
At first I wondered what the words might mean
That thus so strangely found by me had been;
"I take life", yea 'twere easy to perceive
The truth of that, its history I could weave,
And fancy shewed me many a life laid low,
And Death swift summoned by its sudden blow -
Perchance a mother left to mourn the end
Of son, or sorrowing wife her hair to rend
In mad despair, no more to see that face
Whose image Time's own sythe could not erase -
But what was meant by giving life, indeed
T'was strange such words upon a sword to read;
But as I turned the riddle o'er again
Its meaning sudden thrilled my wond'ring brain -
The clashing sword is but the funeral knell
Unto the vanquished, but if wielded well
By stout right arm, to him indeed 'tis life,
'Tis safety and safe passage through the strife -

Thus did I read the riddle, and how true
The hand that erstwhile bore it only knew,
As waving it on high with fist clenched tight
He felt his life protected through the fight -
But all things perish! sad indeed the thought
That he who long ago so valiant fought
Has now been turned to ash and dust,
While this poor sword is left to rot and rust -
Thus musing on far out the brand I cast
Amid the waters as they hurried past;
A sudden splash, a widening ring, no more,
And then the tide rushed onward as before -
There in the river bed perchance t'will stay
For age on age until the judgement day;
Or else like me some other man may find
This old time brand and straight with musing mind,
(Since History in its forge doth oft recast
The deeds almost forgot of days long past;)
Around it such another tale devize
As I have done in solitary wise ---.

---- o ----

"The Legend of St Keyna"

*E*re ever man's defiling hand
Had left its mark upon the land,
Or fallow earth had felt the plough
Returning fruit for sweat of brow;
While nature rested innocent
And undisturbed her tenement;
A spot o'er wooded lay beside
The windings of the Avon's tide -
In later days the axe outrang
And from its blows a village sprang -
Again a time and then a town
Out of the teeming land had grown;
An abbey fair surmounted all
When rang at eve the curfew call;
A master craftsman's tracery,
O'er nature mankind's mastery -
But ne'er a town had ever sprung,
Where long ago the woodlands hung
In groves nigh Avon's banks, had fate
Not destined here a kindlier state.

···········

Keyna, a virgin undefiled,
At Brychan was the only child;
A mighty ruler was her sire,
The ancient King of Brecknockshire -
Pure and fair as the snow was she,
A spur to Knightly rivalry -
Full many a suitor in her train
Could ever court the Lady Keyn -

Princes and Lords undaunted tried
To gain the maiden as a bride;
But nought to all had she to say,
They one and all were sent away -
Deeply her father pondered oft
The reason every suit she scoffed,
Then asked, unable to discern,
Why thus each offer she should spurn -
With drooping eyes that glanced afraid
In accents soft replied the maid:-
"My father, if thou bidst me wed,
"Thy will is law, I bow my head;
"If to my quest thou sayest "nay"
"Nought fear thee but I will obey -
"But this my wish is, that I praise
"Our Lady all my earthly days,
" And live a virgin till I die
"My mortal flesh to mortify -
"To God, and to our Saviour Lord
"And Mary evermore adored,
"My life I long to dedicate,
"And dwell alone my end to wait -
"Shoulds't thou be willing, I intend
"O'er Severn's stream my way to wend,
"And in the woodlands of the west
"Mid solitudes remote to rest -
"Thus trust I by a holy life,
"Shut off from man and earthly strife,
"In Heaven with my God to sit
"As promised by his Holy Writ -
"Thou knowest how from Arthur's Court
"Full many a Knight the Grail have sought;
"Through perils oft have eager passed

"With nought but failure at the last;
"Fearing no thought of ill or pain,
"Esteeming even death a gain -
"Then, father, tell me, why should I
"Not vow a life of purity,
"And wander forth in virgin gown
"If thus I gain a heavenly crown?"
She Paused: her father in amaze
Silent before her steadfast gaze
Made no reply, but stood apart
Sore questioning his aching heart -
At length he raised his hoary head,
Then to the maid in answer said:-
"My child, my heart is very full;
"Feel I as some poor useless hull
"Whose mast is broken; thou hast been
"A staff to me on which to lean -
"Far be it from me to refuse
"Thy asking, or thyself abuse,
"God to me gave thee, lo! I lift
"My praises to him for the gift;
"But God has placed within thy heart
"This wish of thine to live apart;
"Rest thou in him and in his Son;
"Do as thou will - God's will be done -"
Thus kindly spake he, tears full sore
The while a'down his cheeks did pour;
The maid her sire those tears to dry
Caressed in loving sympathy,
And tried to still his heart wrung moan,
By mingling kisses with his own -
At length, more calm, his child he blessed,
Once more unto his bosom pressed,

Then bade her straightway forth to go
Unto such place as God should shew -

....

Across the Severn Keyna went,
Her head in meditation bent;
And on through many a dreary place,
Safe guarded by our Saviour's grace -
Then after wandering days on days,
Through devious and untrodden ways,
By flood and moor, at length she came
Where Keynsham still retains her name -
A dell o'erflowered and wooded round
Whose foliage all the prospect crowned
Lay to a spring, as crystal clear,
With ever welling waters, near -
In undulating pastures fell
The land away beneath the dell,
To where with scintillating gleam
Flowed ceaseless on the Avon's stream -
Bedecked with flowers of every hue,
Of freshest green the grasses too;
The spot wore nature's fairest dress
As loving touched by her caress -
A very Paradise on earth
No barren spot or sign of dearth;
While everything to prove seemed bent
Fond nature all omnipotent -
The Lady Keyna happed by chance
Upon this lovely spot to glance;
Tired were her feet, and travel stained
Her garb, as she the well side gained -
But ere she of the waters drank,

Down down upon the sward she sank,
With bended knee upon the sod,
And praises offered to her God -
Upon her face and hair the dust
Of travel lay in grimy crust;
Her hands were scarred where every thorn
Her tender flesh had rudely torn;
Yet still her eyes with ardour shone
Though blinded by the burning sun -
Then took she water from the pool
Her face and eyes to bathe and cool -
But mindful of a future race,
Filled with the Spirit's holy grace,
Feeling her limbs refreshed again,
Her body healed and cured all pain;
The virgin blessed the lympid well;
And since that day traditions tell
That whensoever man may please,
His eyes afflicted with disease,
To humble come and penitent,
With bearing pure and innocent,
Straight may he drive away his ill
By bathing at the sacred rill -
The Lady kneeling still the same
Laved once again her weary frame,
And quaffed she of the waters, deep,
Then soft composed herself in sleep -
But night brought change; from all around
Arose a sibilant hissing sound;
Effulgent gleams that moved and swayed
About her slumbering body strayed;
As though bright gems unnumbered hung
Each quivering blade of grass among;

Strange sinuous shapes in horrid coils
Embraced her limbs in slimy toils;
Snakes were they, many a venomed asp
Shackled her in their dreadful clasp;
An earthly Paradise indeed,
The heritage of Adam's seed;
A sepulchre of dark despair,
Which outwardly had shewn so fair -
Calm from her sleep the maiden woke,
Shewing no fear as forth she spoke
And lifted up a humble prayer,
Trusting in God's almighty care -
"O God ", she cried "who rulest all,
"Within whose care are great and small,
"If it should please thee that I die,
"Take me to dwell with thee on high;
"But if thou willest that I live,
"O of thy grace and glory give
"To me the power that is thine own
"To turn these serpents into stone -
"Thou gav'st my life, 'tis thine to take;
"Thy will be done: for Christ his sake".
Thus praying, back the maiden reclined,
Her spirit, unto death resigned;
When lo! a wondrous thing occurred,
Within her ears a Voice she heard
In tones ineffable proclaim:-
"Thou who does ask in Christ's own name,
"Thy prayer is answered, give the praise
"To God through all thy earthly days" -
Ere scarce the words had ceased to thrill
The message of God's potent will,
Uncoiled the serpents from her frame

Returning swift from whence they came -
But bare a stonesthrow had they sped,
When all in sickening heaps lay dead;
No sooner they in death lay prone,
Than one and all were turned to stone;
And where so short before had been
So dread and horrible a scene,
Now nought remained with care to cart,
Save only stones the spot to mark -
Later for that she had no stain,
A saint men called the Lady Keyn;
A very saint indeed was she
Who wonders worked by purity -
Now ploughmen tilling up the soil
Will sudden pause within their toil,
And lift a stone, like serpent made,
Which chanced to strike the ploughshare's blade,
Then quick recall the legend old
From sire to sire unending told,
And bless St Keyn with bated breath
For that she did the snakes to death,
And gave a fruitful land and well
To men nigh which secure to dwell.

---- o ----

"St Keyna is storied to have lived here
"(at Keynsham) in a wood infested with
"venomous serpents, and to have converted
"them into stone; and the common people
"long believed that ammonites found
"in the neighbouring quarries, were
"veritable quondam serpents -"

Taken from page 1095 of the Imperial Gazetteer of England and Wales - Vol.III

"Man"

Man the poor paradox,
Single, collective;
Evidence of a God's
Bitter invective -

Dragging his course through life,
Steps slow and leaden;
Weighted with Adam's curse,
Seeking an Eden -

Born in the midst of pain,
Into life tumbled;
Bound with an earthly chain,
Hustled and humbled -

Living from hand to mouth,
Preyed on and preying;
Midst the world's foetid slough
Oftentimes straying -

All through his earthly life
Cares, worries, troubles,
Joys that are joys no more,
Fragile as bubbles -

Creature of circumstance,
Hurried and harried;
Never a pleasing plan
But has miscarried -

One day may nature smile,
Next she is frowning;
Gall comes e'en when Success
His path is crowning -

Feeling the world is vain,
All friends and fickle;
Life's sweetest moments fall
Under death's sickle -

Bitterness, bitterness,
Salt and its savour;
All disappointment but
Give joys their flavour -

Striving to clear his path
Where weeds are showing,
Only still more to find
Before him growing -

Thinking himself a god,
Himself exalting
If he be rich; but poor
Humble and halting -

Hope and hope's satellites
Him onward goading;
Ever his aching back
With troubles loading -

Should but the clouds ahead
Instant be riven,
'Tis a brief glimpse to thee,
Struggler for Heaven -

Called by a paradox,
(Language elastic)
Civilised, (can there be
Word more sarcastic -)

Purex his savage life,
Thousand the pities
That man for greed or gain
Crowded the cities -

Speck in the woof of Time,
Scar on perfection;
Rudderless, sport of fate,
Kismet's direction -

Waiting for nemesis
Juggernaut crashing
Death in unending stream
Over him dashing -

Time's cycles rolling on
Grinding him under
Aeon on aeon pass
Worlds burst asunder -

When may the climax come
Is this eternal?
Will Sethe end it, or
Ages infernal?

All men the same again,
(Cover to cover)
Live through, until the cup
In death runs over -

---- o ----

"A Vision"

Methought I stood upon a moor at night,
Alone, and weighted with a nameless fright;
Upon a spot unhallowed, drear and dank,
From which the mind in chilling horror shrank -
To left to right the land lay desolate,
A dreary stretch of broken slag and slate,
As though fond nature had herself denied,
And stayed her bounteous hand on every side;
While elsewhere showering beauty without spare,
Here for comparison this place left bare -
A solitude uncanny, waste on waste
My shrinking form in all directions faced,
As by some flaming breath in anger seared;
Of slightest sign of vegetation cleared -
Horizon none! an endless track the glance
Could follow ever o'er the vast expanse -
A road unbroken, one way only ploughed,
As by the passing of a ceaseless crowd;
And pointed forward all the prints of feet,
No trace of any hurrying steps retreat -
Then sudden fell from off my eyes the scales,
But of the scene disclosed description fails -
A ceaseless multitude, child, woman, man,
Along the pass with stumbling footsteps ran -
A silent train, with haggard evil face,
Branded with crime and uttermost disgrace -
Degraded, every sense of honor lost,
Mindful too late of sin's infernal cost -
And as I gazed upon this awful tide
Their feet I marked seemed less to walk than glide,
As though some magnet drew unseen along,

Howe'er unwilling, all this ceaseless throng;
And hurled them ever forward on the track,
With no retreat or chance of turning back -
A lowering scudding sky skimmed overhead;
The wind with eerie shrieks the stream of dead,
(For such were they,) encircled round and round,
And like a dirge shrilled forth its wailing sound -
Weird carrion birds swooped down with raucous scream,
Their eyes effulgent with a murd'rous gleam -
Their dripping beaks still gaping open wide,
As if with carnal meals not satisfied -
And followed nigh the strugglers on to hell
With seeming longing for their souls as well;
Though glutted with the mortal body's meal
Yet jealous wishing e'en the wraith to steal,
In order quite their bellies to replete,
And of hell's doom the damnéd soul to cheat -
On, on, still on, in never ceasing mass,
Without distinction, difference or class,
Lowly and rich in life, but now a mob
In death, united by a common sob;
A low drawn cry of anguish, moaning deep,
With eyes that long yet find they cannot weep -
Each of the myriad with his damnéd soul
Unwilling onward hasting to the goal,
The goal of hell, which cavernous before
Awaits with endless tortures evermore -
No more I witnessed, screaming with affright
I dashed away, and left th'accursed sight;
Then safe again uncovered swift my head,
And praises offered that among these dead,
Which to their awful doom thus onward race,
Appeared for me within their ranks no place -

---- o ----

Life. ---- and Death

Why do we live? Why breathe the breath of life
Within so dark an atmosphere of strife,
And why submit, while o'er us rudely clangs
The knell to joy, the call for endless pangs?
Why struggle on, our eyes obscure of sight,
Amid a world where might is ever right;
Where garish spleandour, riches, outward show,
But scarcely hide the skeleton below?
Why not obey the impatient call within,
The spirit beating 'gainst the bars of sin?
Why not at once life's fearsome struggle cease,
And then in death the eager soul release;
The soul that like a bubble strives to rise
Amid the ooze that thick around it lies;
A bubble that like life at length will burst,
And in the air of Heaven be dispersed?
What reason is there for this endless toil,
This everlasting turning of the soil;
These Herculean labours day by day,
This ceaseless working of a mortal clay?
Why may not man die out upon this globe,
And wrap his weary head in Sethe's robe?
Ay! why not at his will be swept aside,
And unto death at one short moment glide?
But hark the answer! Man has not the will
To die; at one swift stroke his life to still;
He knows not why, though longing for the end,
Against himself his hand he cannot bend;
However crushed he rarely welcomes death
Or draws with joyful heart his dying breath -

What feeling is this, instinct rooted deep,
That makes him for his life such fondness keep?
Why should the love of life exist so strong
To drive him all his earthly days along,
And to a shadow a chimaera cling
That ever trouble in its train will bring?
We feeble mortals with our blinded eyes
Can only wonder, make a poor surmise,
And marvel what good purpose we fulfil
By ever stumbling up life's rugged hill -
What reason could have predisposed a God
To fashion into man a mass of clod?
A God omnipotent whose very face
Is deeply shrouded from the human race;
Whose actions are a mystery to men,
His ways, his thoughts, beyond their feeble ken -
The Godhead is to man as much unknown
As whence that body, which he calls his own
Has come; what purpose gave it first its breath,
What purpose summons it unwilled to death -
Has this great Being in our nature placed
The love of life, which time has not effaced,
That man continue on this earth to breed,
To fructify, perpetuate his seed,
Until such time as God in wondrous tone
Of satisfaction owns his work is done?
Or is God's purpose so in life to scourge
The earthly body and the soul to purge,
Until the soul is cleansed and purely bright
Fit to appear in God's own holy sight?
'Tis all but idle surmise; none can tell
The purposes that cause our hearts to swell,
The love of life so strongly to exist,

When all around is but a foetid mist,
A slough of bitterness, of dull despair,
A charnel house of crime, a world of care,
A struggle hard enough with which to cope
Without the mirage of deferred hope -
This hope for better things that ceaseless drives
Us onward through the turmoil of our lives;
This hope fulfilment which but rarely brings,
But further failure in our faces flings -
This hope forlorn which rings so sweet a sound,
But ever bitter to the taste is found;
This hope, a spirit, evanescent wraith,
Whose cringing satellite in life is faith -
Faith! preachers bid us down before it cower,
To bind ourselves unasking to its power;
To heed nought else but through the world's mad fight
To keep it as our banner still in sight;
Although no help therefrom in life we see,
Yet when the soul is from the body free,
T'will so they scream to Heaven's portals soar,
And with its God be cherished evermore -
Faith! only glance on every side around;
Mark how the chain of earth is tightly bound
To every morbid struggler, hearts long dead
In more material toil for daily bread -
What time have they for faith? Their sluggish feet
Are clogged with worldly mire as down they beat
Upon the track of sin, with eyes that glance
At every other spawn of hell askance -
Each fears the other ever seeks to snatch
His gains, and thus he keeps untiming watch;
Like some poor dog that snarls beside a bone,
And guards until he thinks himself alone;

Then buries it that others may not take
What he wants not, but cares not to forsake -
Faith! Can you find it? E'en the child but bears
Perhaps a morsel for a few short years,
Then mixing on a sudden with the world,
Straight is that faith down to oblivion hurled -
A lover when his heart with love first sighs,
Sees nought but beauty in his lady's eyes,
And perfect faith each for the other holds,
While each their nature to the other moulds;
But disillusionment full soon is seen,
The king has fallen, she no more is queen,
And faith which for a time had reigned supreme
Is cast aside as but an empty dream -
No! all is vanity, and hoping vain,
A life of emptiness, a world of pain -
Hope is a siren, singing soft of joys,
And then to deeper depths of woe decoys -
God's purpose is unknown, we all are blind,
The way he wishes never can we find;
So that unanswered is the question still,
Why do we live, what purpose great fulfill?

---- o ----

The Gamin

See yonder lamppost, 'neath its lurid glare
The miserable object standing there;
Watch how he draws his rags about his form,
Striving to guard against the wintry storm -
His clothes in tatters scarcely serve to hide
The limbs beneath; here gaping open wide
In tattered rents; here rudely stitched and patched
With string and bits of cloth most poorly matched -
An urchin of the streets without a home,
In beggarwise compelled about to roam.
Asking his daily bread from door to door,
With prospects equal to the day before -
Perchance into this world unwilling brought
Within the precincts of some squalid court,
Suckled on evil, nurtured up on crime,
Soiled from the first with sin's insidious slime -
Merely a speck upon life's troubled waters,
The bastard breed of England's fallen daughters;
Feeling the want of home, yet knowing none,
Damned from his birth for sin he has not done -
For him the brightest day in life will be
When kindly death his sullied soul sets free;
Still more at birth thrice blest had been the day
Had death his gasping life then snatched away -
Homeless and hungry, oft without a bed
On which at night to lay his aching head;
While when in some retreat at eve he flings
His form, he knows not what the morrow brings;
Holding no hope amid the world's mad strife,
Feeling no care when death may end his life;

Having no knowledge of the wrong from right,
Hating the daytime, longing for the night -
His pleading glance is scorned by passers by
Who view his plight with supercilious eye -
Twisted by tortures of an earthly hell,
His happiest hours are in a prison cell -
He owns a soul, so moralists may say,
Which will be tried upon the Judgement Day;
A soul encrusted thick with sin and guilt,
For which to win a Saviour's blood was spilt -
Did he but know that he could call his own
A soul at least, so evil has he grown,
That Esaulike he'd quickly make a deal,
And sell his birthright for a single meal -
The Pharisees professing him their brother
All outward signs of help strive hard to smother,
And dare him e'en to touch their garment hems,
Insult his poverty, his want condemn -
Within their lavish homes the very waste
Would be to him a king's repast to taste -
They oft refuse a crust of bread to give,
And make him ask what right he has to live -
What wonder if sore pressed by those above
Who thus put far away all Christian love,
That he resenting their attempts to kill,
Steals of the riches which they use so ill -
Yet when convicted in the dock he stands,
The world in righteous wrath holds up its hands,
Ne'er thinking that they were themselves to blame
The lack of giving when for help he came,
Or that perchance he always was bereft
Of knowledge of the moral wrong of theft -
So he lives on; unaided, goaded, spurned,

In the world's whirlpool sadly tossed and churned;
Driven into crime, wanting a helping hand,
A pariah and an outcast in the land -
Who then can wonder that his feeble breath
Of life so soon is tapped and drawn by death.
Unknown he lives an Acherontian slave,
And finds scant burial in a pauper's grave -
Such is you outcast, such his grievous case,
To every Christian nation a disgrace;
His lifetime blighted, Death at hand, and then,
A stain upon the souls of Christian men.

----o----

The Miser's Death

What are these thoughts that trouble me tonight?
Are they the phantoms of another world,
The spirits of the dead come back once more
To stir my conscience to a late remorse?
Here have I lived within this barren room
In poverty and rags for years on years
With nought to please me, save my hoarded gold.
That is the secret - Gold and nought but gold.
How I have striven to attain these heaps
That lie before me, strewn upon the ground
In wild confusion - Who but I could tell
What hours of agony and sweat
These hoards have cost me to accumulate!
Ah! what a talisman in life is gold!
What can be done without it in this world?
It is the key to greatness, to renown,
While every heart throws open wide its gates
In order to receive the lust for wealth,
It is the mighty stepping stone on which
All nations rise and fall, and every man
By means of gold is straightway made or marred -
It is the God, the Saviour of the world -
Ah sweet sweet gold, my life, my soul, my blood,
The very means whereby I draw my breath.
Here have I lying in these glitt'ring heaps
More than the ransom of the greatest King,
Treble the value of a mortal soul!
And as I gain each shining little piece,
It seems as if I added one more drop
Of life to my existence, if I lose

It brings me one step nearer unto death.
What then can woman's paltry charms avail
Against your mighty sway? I live, I feel,
I palpitate with life whene'er I touch
Your shining form, or take you in my hand,
And laugh whilst listening to your chink, chink, chink,
As through my fingers to the ground you slip -
Aha, aha, what powers for good or ill
Your tiny shape to other men might bring,
But I have got you safely in my clutch,
My all in all, in you alone is bound
The very essence of my earthly life -
How I have madly fought and toiled and strived
To gain you, yet with ne'er a single thought
Of pity, or the means which I employed.
Away ye shadows of the murky mist
That come uncalled to haunt me - Long ago
I stilled my conscience, and of no avail
Is it if ye surround me with your forms,
Striving to fright me with your bitter gibes -
What voice is this that whispers in my ear?
I seem to know its tone; ah yes! 'twas hers
Whose blood I shed to gain what wealth she had -
What matters it? Had she but lived, long since
The whole would have been squandered, gone or lost.
What is one life amid the myriad swarms
Of creatures that infest this globe? For gold
Whole nations have gone blithely to their death -
Ha, ha, you trickle through my outsretched hands
Just as her blood dripped down upon the earth -
I grasp you in my fingers, madly clutch
You to my breast, my very soul is rent
For love of you. What music heavenly sweet

Lies in the ring, the clink of ruddy gold -
You look like blood - What tales each piece could tell
Of murder, rapine, war, gold's holocaust-
. . . . .
What is this horror What this sudden change
That comes upon me? Lo! I scarce can see
Your beauteous form, my eyes do sudden seem
Quite dim - What can it mean? It cannot be
That I am growing blind, or far worse still
That madness is about to clutch my brain
As I have clutched my gold - What is this pain
That grips me at the throat? Away, away!
Have pity, leave me to my hardwon wealth,
I ask no more; I cannot live without.
Or is it that the phantom death has come
To claim me for his own. Ah! if 'tis so,
'Tis more than cruel that he comes so soon -
I have not lived as yet one half the span
To men allotted - No! I will not die -
There is no death for me - I will tear back
My life e'en from the very hand of God -
But stay! There is no death there is no God,
Gold is my god. There is no God beside -
Ha, ha, no God! I scream no God but Gold,
Nothing, I say shall part me from my wealth,
Not even Death himself - Away, Away!
Ye spirit phantoms, dare not to approach,
My gold shall awe you. Save me, O my Gold!
God cannot touch me since there is no God,
Neither can Death. I live - Aha - ah...I...

----o----

Death hath no sting.

*I*s life worth living? Gods gigantic jest
In this vast universe was forming man
In his own image - God th'eternal One,
Man the poor puppet, tossed about in life,
Swayed here and there with just sufficient brain
To drive him mad, a passing waif and stray
Scattered amid the flotsam of the world:
Distraught with fears and doubts, with every hope
Predestined to be crushed eternally -
God being perfect laughs at puny man,
His struggles to attain th'impossible,
His Pelion on Ossa like attempts
To gain perfection; ever slipping back,
Like waves upon the shore, which strive to reach
One pebble more, and striving break away
Back to the great expanses of the deep,
There to be straightway lost for evermore -
And yet each wave makes the mighty whole;
While each man's life is as the life of all,
A mighty failure, time antithesis
To God and God's perfection absolute -
The beasts themselves are better off than man;
They have no mind to goad them madly on.
To hope and hope and ne'er be satisfied
Until grim death steps in and ends the farce -

Ah! God is cruel, death alone is Kind,
If death brings but complete oblivion
From all the cares and worries of this life,
And endless sleep be his sole attribute.
No man may taste of pleasure to the full:

Scarce have his lips been wetted, when the cup
Is madly dashed away, and all his soul
Is filled with bitter anguish and regret -
Then why not hate this life and long for Death?
And where can wrong be if a man courts Death,
Ay! even forces it upon himself?
Man had no option given him at birth,
Against his will brought forth, and straightway hurled
Into the turmoil of the world's career;
And with what object, but to die again?
The babe's first instincts cause it to complain
Against the strange injustice of its birth -
Death claims from every mortal his deserts -
Then why be born expecting only death?
'Tis said the spirit from the body freed
Goes straight to God to his own Judgement Seat;
Then every soul must evermore be damned!
The purest mortal when compared with God
Is covered by the canopy of sin,
Making perfection unattainable;
And if not perfect God can ne'er be found -
Then 'twere far better to believe that death
Completes this life with everlasting sleep -
For who would face another life like this,
And still another, till in course of time
The soul should be so purged and purified,
As to be fit to face the Eye of God -
Wherefore God laughs aloud at puny man,
His one mistake amid the Universe -
Then come, O Death, and dying let there be
But death, and death's complete oblivion-

----o----

L'Envoi

*T*hough long the toil, who counts the cost,
Who cries that 'tis love's labours lost
If but a fleeting pleasure
Be yours to whom I send this book,
If mem'ry wake whene'er you look
In moments of your leisure?

Though dead the days these lines inspired,
Though buried is the love that fired
The fancies here recorded;
You only know the meaning deep,
The thoughts that 'neath the surface sleep,
Though oftimes dimly worded –

---- o ----

AFTERTHOUGHT

It has been during the preparation for publishing of these poems that I realised that I might have missed something of significance relating to the mystery of whom this *Carolus* might have been.

I have been suddenly struck with the thought that, bearing in mind his ability to compose such readable and enjoyable *Lyrics & Lines* as contained herein, was it just possible that, having composed these for the *Love that he had now lost,* he had later written many more?

It seems doubtful that having such poetic skill he never put pen to paper again after completing these works - why would someone with such an ability no longer use his undoubted talent to write more such compelling lines? Perhaps he did write more, perhaps he wrote, and published them, under another name, his real name or another pseudonym. Perhaps he wrote more and they have never seen the light of day. Kept tucked away in a box, a bureau draw, in an attic or anywhere and there they still remain even now.

If he wrote more and they were published still begs the question of who was he? If never published and still languishing somewhere perhaps, just perhaps, somewhere out there in the North Eastern corner of the English county of Somerset there is today a family with a draw or box full of poems that came from a now deceased Grand or Great Grandfather who never divulged either the existence of, or for whom he had written, his Lyrics & Lines or that he had identified himself to his lost love as *Carolus*.

JPP/Feb2019